# Oh No,

A gust of wind blows Zeb from a tree.
His friends are worried. Is he hurt?
Read the story to find out how Danny,
Emma and Josh make Zeb better.

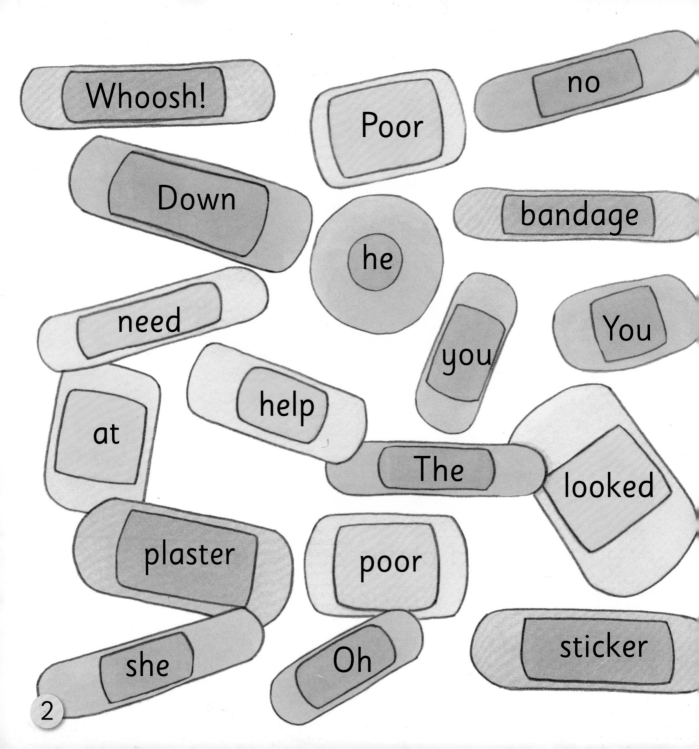

Zeb

Whoosh!
Down went Zeb ... down, down, down.

'Oh no!' said Danny.
'Oh no!' said Emma.
'Oh no!' said Josh.

I am dizzy!

'Poor Zeb,' they said.
'You need help.'

'We can help,' said Danny.

'Hello Zeb,' said Danny.
'We can help you.'

Danny looked at Zeb.
'Poor Zeb,' he said.
'You need a plaster.'

11

Josh looked at Zeb.
'Poor Zeb,' he said.
'You need a big bandage.'

12

The bandage went round and round Zeb.

Emma looked at Zeb.
Zeb looked at Emma.

'Poor Zeb,' she said.
'Poor, poor Zeb.
You need a ...

**... sticker!'**

# Lost!

Danny and Josh and Emma are worried.
Zeb is lost and he must be very sad.
The children will have to find him!
But where can he be?
Read the story and find out where
Zeb is hiding.

'Zeb is lost,' said Danny.
'Oh no!' said Josh.
'Oh no!' said Emma.

'I looked and looked,' said Danny,
'but Zeb is lost.'
'Oh no!' said Emma.
'Poor Zeb,' said Emma. 'He must be sad.'

'Zeb is lost,' said Danny.
'He needs help.
We must find him.'

Off they went.

'Hello parrot,' said Emma.
'Zeb is lost. Can you help us please?'
'Squawk!' said the parrot and off he went.

'Hello monkey,' said Danny.
'Zeb is lost. Can you help us please?'
'Eek! Eek!' said the monkey and off he went.

Ssss!

'Hello snake,' said Josh.
'Zeb is lost. Can you help us please?'
'Ssss!' said the snake and off he went.

'Poor Zeb,' said Emma. 'He must be sad.'
'Zeb is sad,' said Josh, 'and we are sad,
very, very sad.'
'We must find him!' said Danny.

Off they went.
They looked and looked and looked.

They saw Zeb!

'Hello Zeb,' said Danny. 'You are not sad.
You are happy, very, very happy!'
'Zeb is happy and we are happy,'
they said, 'very, very happy.'

Danny and Josh and Emma went home.

'Hello parrot,' said Mum.
'Hello monkey.'
'Hello snake.'
'Hello Zeb,' she said. 'You are happy,
very, very happy, but you need ...

… a wash!'